AF483927

Tulipwood Books | Seattle, WA
tulipwood.org

Published 2024 by Tulipwood Books
Printed in the United States of America

Edited and Designed by Lynne Ellis
Cover photo: "Earth Breath" by AJ Dent

First Edition

ISBN: 979-8-9914048-1-5

seedfall

volume one

Tulipwood Books | 2024

contents

K Janeschek

9 The First Hunt
10 Undoing Darkness

Jude Wineke

11 Stardust

Christina Ana Montilla

14 My Soulmate is Stuck on the International Space Station
15 Tsuchinshan-ATLAS

Marissa Bea

16 Donny and Michelle

AJ Dent

19 Frost Froth
20 Festival Sylphs

Alli Parrett

21 Uncentered

Shanda Connolly

34 New Moon in Aries

Lydia McDermott

35 Big Muffett

Courtney Bambrick

36 Instructions for Needles and Pins

Harper Walton

37   Daisies

Vivian Li

38   Be Guāi-et

Erin Armstrong

41   The Wrestling Match

Michelle Herman

44   Sea-Change

Mikun Oluwayemi

54   Remember
55   Watch Me
56   Even Flowers Cast a Black Shadow

Deborah Bacharach

57   How to Pray

Carrie Redway

58   Father Jupiter

Abby E. Murray

60   Grief in December
62   How Not to Be a Buzzkill at Holiday Gatherings
64   A Fact About Trees

Ambalila Hemsell

65   love song for the ocean
66   wildfire

Dear Reader,

Welcome to the first issue of *seedfall*, a new journal of poetry, prose, and visual art. I'm so happy that we're here together.

In the summer of 2024, I had an idea. The project: to reimagine the way that books are produced. Frustrated by the conflation of poetry and product in some corners of the literary world, I imagined a press that would lean into the art and the writer as its supporting structures.

I'm writing to you from the first day after the U.S. electorate made it known to the world that, in the majority, we have become a nation that values selfishness and fear over equality and trust. We now have a president-elect who has repeatedly shown his bias for the needs of the privileged few over the needs of the many. You know the rest. It's all over the news.

I'm desperately sad for my country.

With the clarity of this grief comes purpose: recommit to a joy that coexists with anger. As I sit in my new chair at Tulipwood Books, I want to promise that I am here to support you. I will never make you change your voice for anyone—whether politician, family member, lit mag reader, teacher, or patron. You are valuable, just as you are. I am your collaborator and superfan, and I know that you can create beauty in this unjust world.

In this issue you'll find thoughtful, revolutionary work by writers and artists: Abby E. Murray, AJ Dent, Alli Parrett, Ambalila Hemsell, Carrie Redway, Christina Ana Montilla, Courtney Bambrick, Deborah Bacharach, Erin Armstrong, Harper Walton, Jude Wineke, K Janeschek, Lydia McDermott, Marissa Bea, Michelle Herman, Mikun Oluwayemi, Shanda Connolly, and Vivian Li. Most of these pieces were originally accepted for a different journal: *Papeachu Review Six: Atmosphere*.

So: what happened to Papeachu?

Nothing dramatic.

After Meg moved to Spain we kept the press going and published two additional books. Eventually, the time zone difference and geographical distance proved too big of a challenge and, with sadness, we decided to slowly wind down.

Meg taught me—in a way that no one else in my sphere of influence had ever articulated—that the human behind the work is the most important thing about the art. I'm doing my best to carry that philosophy forward.

I want to thank the contributors to *Atmosphere* for allowing me to publish their work under the Tulipwood Books imprint. As a working poet myself, I know how meaningful each piece that we write is—and I understand the hours and hours of work that go into taking an idea from the mind and placing it on the page. Your trust is an inspiration to me, and it's powering my own creation engine right now.

Your work is a zephyr to everyone who sees and reads it.

Please look for hope in these pages: here is the hope of atmospheric phenomena, celestial objects, space travel, inevitable mortality, new relationship energy; of how to work with your hands, how to stand solid and true, to discover and rediscover and embrace the self, to care for family, to connect through art and language, connect to the spiritual; how to grieve and grieve and bring the grief out into the open, to question, to allow the wind in, to live on the same planet as the octopus, to bathe in the knowledge that our species is temporary—that our own lives are fragile and finite—and that it makes us extraordinary.

So what do we do now? We read books. We read new books. We read banned books. We give books to our children and our friends' children. We read books written in free languages and in the language of the oppressor, and we learn to cast curses and spells in those languages. And we write.

In community,

Lynne Ellis

K Janeschek

The First Hunt

I heard a silence the other night. On a cold hill,
before the great emptiness of sky and snow.
There were lights. Low, green. I realized that I want
to know the world more, not less. Even if
it splinters me from the river beneath the bridge.
Even if my breath does not have time to gather before
it falls to the ground, hard. It was colder
in that valley after sound abandoned us—the earth
nibbled at my toes. Stillness caught the wind.
Before then, I had never watched a light die
and waited in the dark for its return.

Undoing Darkness

You pull over the car at your spot.
You're grizzled now—you have territory,
land that takes you close to the sky, and you look up
solar winds ahead of time. When that first green
thread appears, your girlfriend
is still fiddling with her camera, her fingers
already numb to the wind, nearly
bitten. Though used to the bitterness, it catches
you now, chokes you most when the sky is singing.
Singing? No, this is not a song, not even
a dance. This is a ripple, a pulse, a bleed
of light coming across great emptiness. A reminder that
there is more to the night than stars
needling the dark. For as long as the sky
is alive and on fire, you snap
pictures with your phone. Then, silence.
The sky's scream burns brief behind your eyelids.
As if night was only a dark cloud,
the world stills. You and your girlfriend
get back in your car, drive the long way
home past the fields and the lone barn, a gray hull
before white endlessness. Later, you watch
the snow come down and think: *how gently this
ash falls to earth.*

Jude Wineke

Stardust

SPACE WAS COLD, AND it had a taste. The only way he could think to describe it was the sharpness of a tiled bathroom in the thick of winter. He'd never set foot in one, but he could imagine the running faucet and the thin strips of grout between the squares of white.

Earth was blurry from far away, but nice. The crash of cresting white caps and knobbly forests of broken branches faded into a gently swirling patchwork quilt somewhere between brown and blue.

He liked to roll onto his back when he fell asleep, the stars gathered up to his chin like white-hot stitches on a duvet, and let their voices lull him like white noise. He remembered the first time he heard a human voice, once just an itch of a thought of a hope suddenly a guttural roar of a word. It was a strange thing to accept from the small, waxen things he'd watched clamber across rocks and point at him with the jab of a crooked, hairy thumb. Still, he took it.

They talked a lot of loneliness, the people.

They didn't shout of it, it was a whisper offered up between cupped hands instead of spat on an open palm.

They kept it to themselves like pictures in lockets or family heirlooms on high shelves. It was something to be felt, some presence to wallow in silently, some specter only to be recognized when it broke, when it fell, when it demanded to be noticed.

Loneliness was something he contemplated with his eyes closed.

It was an ache that deepened in the stagnant hours as he slipped through the icy curtain of blackness, an ache that sharpened with each revolution around the sun.

Sometimes, when his eyes refused to shut, he'd flip onto his stomach and stare into the sun until his eyes went white. Every few hundred years, when he coasted close enough to it that it seared his face and peeled off the layers of ice and rock he'd sweated in for decades, he would consider diving headfirst into its great yellow depths. Rattle around like dice in a cup. Melt to the dust he'd been before gravity had beaded him together. Curl into himself until he was so small he was hardly more than a shriveled human fist.

He couldn't remember what he'd been before he was this, or if he'd been something more before each revolution shaved off a slice of his newly assembled body. Maybe a marvel, or maybe just a bigger hunk of stone and ice and metal.

One day, he woke up stripped bare, melted to rock ribs and gnarled icicle toenails, cheeks hollow and lips peeling. He screamed, and it curled out between his lips in a protracted exhale. He scrambled, tangling end over end.

Sun, earth.

Sun, earth.

Space.

He closed his eyes to enter a blackness that was his, but they had turned to butterfly wings. Tears streamed up his body, catching in the hollows behind joints and wandering into the depressions cradling organs.

Up and up, snot and spit, draining draining draining.

The voices blurred as he hurtled, a radio station set to static.

Isn't it strange to want and then for reality to melt popsicle down to stick, and you're gnashing your teeth at splintered wood.

He was fetal, quivering lips pressed against his navel.

Earth was warm, and it had a taste. The only way he could think to describe it was the grit of cinnamon toothpaste warmed by morning breath.

He stared up, his duvet unspooled and smeared across the sky in little clusters. There was the familiar darkness with its puncture holes. There was the moon, the great big hole punch.

His ears were full of a thousand tiny bells. He pawed at them with his toothpick fingers, but the ringing did not abate. He felt glued to the dirt, some interminable force draped across him like a wanting lover. Every breath clattered in his lungs.

Something broke through his trance: some crunch of disturbed earth, some displacement of breeze. He was rising, back arched and head thrown back.

He stared up, and two gaping holes and their persistent deluge of air answered. A gash opened wide and dozens of shiny teeth winked in the moonlight. The ringing deafened, now a spiked band across his head.

He dropped into a cavern of denim, pressed tight to warmth. He reached out, searching. There was something hard and silver, there was a dryer-warmed receipt.

He dreamed of nothing as he jostled, exhausted by the cataclysm of sound.

He awoke on a shelf. He studied the white tile with thin strips of grout. He studied the uncapped cinnamon toothpaste spilling its contents onto the water-slick sink. The silence was a pressure.

He missed his wide open sky, he missed his firefly sun. He longed for the weightlessness and his ever-moving body. He closed his eyes, the taste of space lingering on his tongue, and thought of loneliness.　■

Christina Ana Montilla

My Soulmate is Stuck on the International Space Station

after Bader AlAwadhi

Every ember exploded at once.
Every orbit could be calculated.
Everything is fine.
The word "every" is a determiner.
"Every" is used to indicate something happening
At specified intervals.
Every family has a lost one.
"Every" is used to emphasize, to be an utmost.
Not every religion believes in soulmates.
"A mate to your soul," clarifies Zea.
For instance: the religion of frogs does not.
Frogs can get themselves out of most misfortune, but not every.
Everything Everywhere All at Once is a very fine movie.
Every astronaut is required to watch it.
Is required to watch Time Collapse As It Does
In that movie. Every astronaut is required
To rank each family member
On a piece of paper, a "Yes, call in case of
Emergency" to "No,
Please don't call" list.
My aunt Connie is as fragile as a railroad
Spike; yes, call her.
Grandma is with the moths
At the darkened porch light. She used to tell me
Never trust a man, he'd do worse
Than take your last nickel.
Proving money can't buy heartbreak.
The nickel is a fine excuse for the cold moon
Tonight; he fits in my pocket.
Every pocket has a man.
Every night has a lost one.

Tsuchinshan-ATLAS

We never saw the comet.
We never looked for it.
We set an alarm for dusk.
Where the comet winked brightest, southwest smile.
The alarm went off.
We never broke away.
We never set the alarm.
We never broke attention.
To break would have broken.
We never saw what was coming for us
Forty-four million miles away.

Marissa Bea

Donny and Michelle

IT WAS DECEMBER, AND THEY FLEW above the pillowy clouds. Twelve thousand feet would be just high enough. The skies were unusually blue and bright, as if the planet was forgiving the human race for all its transgressions, allowing one last beautiful morning to awe at the only place they had ever called home. They sat in the cockpit in silence, Donny focusing his hardest on keeping them in the air, even though the ride was as smooth as he'd ever experienced. Michelle's eyes melted over him, and she smiled, her joyful memories leaving a prickly sensation on the top of her skin.

He had been flying since he was fourteen. His grandfather had told him that flying would get him "in" with "the ladies." As a love-drunk teenager, that had been appealing to Donny. He had flown private charters for celebrities, tours for rich families, and did a brief stint ferrying unmarked packages around the country. He still didn't know what had been in those boxes. Michelle always said it was probably dolls filled with various illegal sundries. She loved that he was an adventurer and possibly a criminal.

They had met twenty years prior, when she accidentally sat on his blanket at a meteor shower event, thinking it belonged to her friends, and she never left. They found out that they were both on the list to send average people on a one-way trip to Mars, but once the meteor was discovered, NASA had canceled the program. But most of life went on as usual; humanity demanded consistency (or possibly willful denial). Every other Saturday they would wake up and make their way to the planetarium to sit alongside students and families and listen to the stories of the heavens. They donated to space exploration societies and attended panel discussions about the likelihood of bacterial life on Europa and Ganymede. They never missed an eclipse.

When the final days arrived, everyone in their families carried out their respective, separate plans. They had spent a year saying all their goodbyes to each other. Michelle's sister and her husband drove off into the desert. Her parents loved watching soccer, so they turned on recorded reruns of great games and planned to scream profanities at the referees. Donny's children and grandchildren all sat together with their partners at a long wooden table that had been carved from an ancient tree, celebrating the life they had been granted with a full feast, wine, and music.

Donny timed their takeoff to the second. NASA had made it known exactly what day and time the meteor would hit, and they knew they wouldn't be the only ones in the air that day. Hundreds of other planes were soaring the local skies, speckling the blue like confetti, people inside preparing for their final moments. Pockmarks of love in flight.

The roar of the engines rang in their ears as they looked into each other's eyes and smiled. The love no longer needed to be spoken. It could be seen in every crease, every spot, felt with every year behind them. Donny had watched Michelle's hair match his gray over time, her blue eyes growing lighter and softer, while his had deepened to the darkest brown.

Their foreheads came together for a brief moment before they clasped hands and tilted sideways from the plane out into nothingness. Their fingers held fast, their knuckles like steel, gravity pulling them infinitely closer to the earth and each other. Their free fall paused as the shockwave passed, lifting them back up toward the atmosphere. The blooming fireball in the distance seemed to move in slow motion, its dark base a pedestal for the ombré of reds and oranges leading up to the yellow and white pinnacle. The bright light that snuffs one adventure only to begin another. They could feel the warmth arriving.

Michelle spun her back to Donny, fitting her cheek next to his, and they embraced one last time before their vapor was returned to the stars they both loved so well. ∎

Dear Reader,

this space is for your words.

AJ Dent

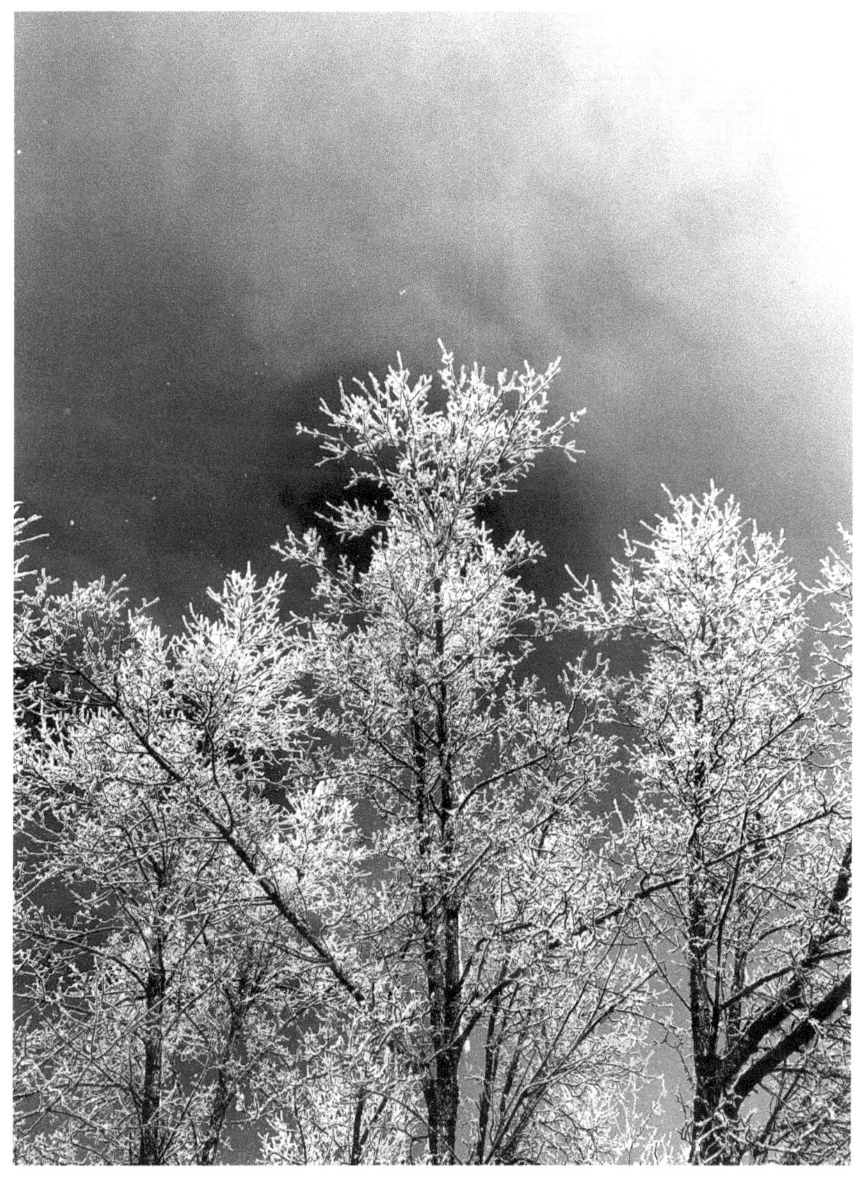

Frost Froth

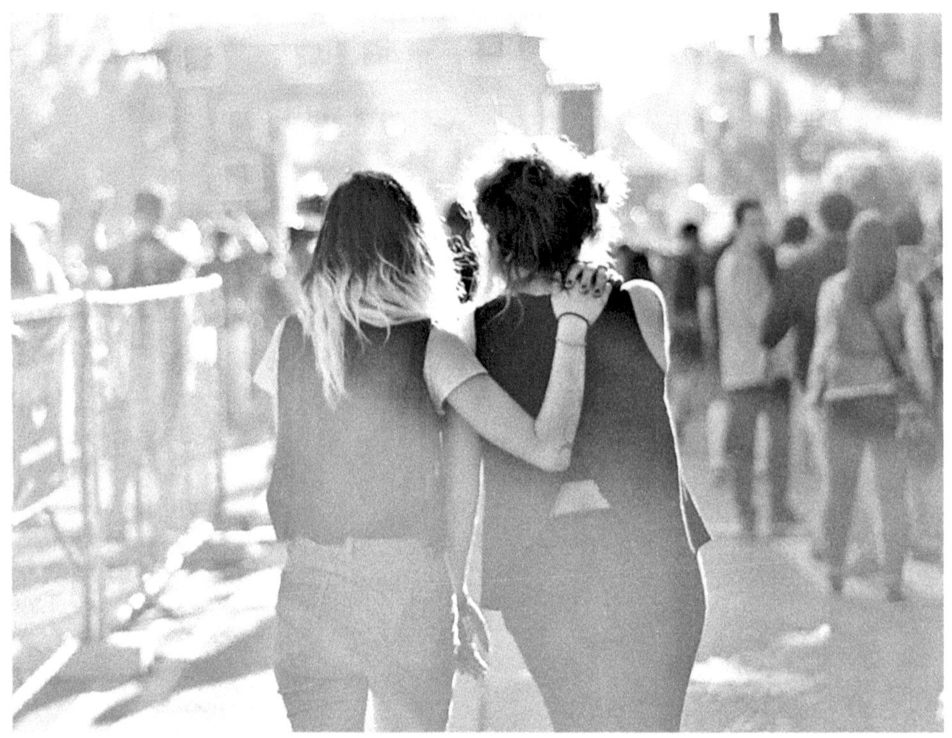

Festival Sylphs

Alli Parrett

Uncentered

THE BAR IS DIMLY LIT and not too loud. Paige doesn't see Marlee. She walks up to the bar, careful to find a spacious spot so she doesn't transfer clay dust to someone else's dry-clean-only ensemble.

The prices are higher than bars she frequents, though there aren't many. When she does drink, it is at home with her roommates and over a shared meal. Being a working artist doesn't afford the luxury of Seattle's artisanal, farm-to-table, locally-sourced nightlife. Instead, her livelihood is funded by those that can afford such things.

"I wasn't sure if you'd show up." Marlee's voice is quiet and close. She looks more professional than when they were at the studio.

"Neither was I." Paige still isn't sure of herself. Even under hushed lights, Paige is exposed—surrounded by type A business and finance professionals privy to her date, free to scrutinize and gossip.

"Let me buy you a drink." Marlee steps closer, wedging in at the bar, unconcerned by the clay dust on Paige. "What would you like?"

"A cider would be great." The words escape Paige's mouth as if they are a single word. "Thanks," she says.

Like Paige's favorite glaze, Marlee's hazel eyes are speckled with greens and ambers like a forest floor. The melding of inspiration and uncertainty roil in Paige's mind.

Marlee orders herself a gin and tonic with an extra lime. They clink glasses and take a sip. Paige feels Marlee's eyes on her the entire time.

For the first drink, they talk about long-ago college majors—ceramics and psychology, respectively—family origins—only child and one of four—their careers—an enjoyable struggle and rewarding. Paige has never talked to a psychologist before. While they talk, she finds herself being cautious of her words.

Paige buys the second round.

A server taps Marlee's shoulder. "Your table is ready," he says so only the two of them can hear him.

Marlee looks at Paige. "I made a reservation just in case," she says.

Paige can see she's excited but doesn't want to be pushy.

"Would you want to join me for dinner?"

Sweat wells in the creases of Paige's palms. She kneads her fingers, turning residual dust into tiny beads of clay.

•

AT EACH WHEEL, PAIGE PLACES a small bucket filled with a sponge and tools. In moments when her hands are empty, her fingers tap along to the music that floods the studio. The music varies from day to day based on the resident artist that is running a class. On Paige's class days, it is always grunge or something similar. The other artists think it's too cliché for Seattle.

Paige is counting down the minutes, but when the door creaks on its hinges, she jumps. A cohort of four: Marlee, Ned, and the Jacksons.

"Our marriage counselor thinks it would be good for us to explore a hobby together," Mrs. Jackson offers to Paige, and consequentially the other students.

"We'll see," Mr. Jackson mutters.

The silence grows thick while everyone exchanges tense glances. Paige mumbles a welcome and something about everyone being there to learn. "There's aprons if you want one," she says, pointing to the hooks on the wall.

Ned and the Jacksons look at her clay-saturated jeans and opt to protect their own clothing. Marlee, however, takes her place at a wheel.

"I don't mind getting messy," Marlee says. She pulls up her mostly-black hair into a tight but messy bun. From her temples, silver strands peek through. Marlee folds her hands in her lap while she waits for everyone else to join her.

In the eight years of teaching beginner's pottery, Paige has never had someone welcome the mess that clay creates.

The introduction to a new class goes the same every time. Paige has her script memorized. Explain the three-session class structure, point out each station, demonstrate wedging the clay, walk them through the functions of the potter's wheel, and show them how to center the clay. This is the part that everyone wants to get to anyways. Back when Paige taught classes at the community college, she required each student to master each step before they could move onto the next. Clay would be wedged until they produced consistent, air-free mounds of clay. Then center the clay on the wheel until she could push on their arms and shoulders without pushing the clay. Then pull cylinders until the walls were thin and even from the foot to the brim. Consistency is necessary and repetition is the only path. But those were college students that had declared they wanted to pursue the artist path. These students want to make a nice bowl for their friend's birthday.

After watching Paige, each student sits at their wheel, secures their clay in the center, adds water, and presses down on the pedal. Clay splatters in the basins, escaping on occasion to decorate the aprons. Paige watches little flecks of white slip bead on Marlee's plaid flannel and black skinny jeans. A few minutes pass before most of them claim they centered their clay. None of them are without a wobble when the wheel spins, but Paige takes to her own wheel and demonstrates the next step.

She presses her foot to the pedal, getting the wheel turning at a medium speed as she presses her middle finger into the center of the clay, stopping a centimeter or so before the bottom before she pulls her finger towards her to open the center. Paige doesn't usually take notice of the students when she demos but she can feel each time Marlee leans in or cocks her head to observe the specific motions that she is making. Her muscles begin to tense under Marlee's scrutiny. Paige rushes through the explanation of pulling the walls up and in three fluid motions morphs the stump of clay into a cylinder.

All Apologies hums over the speakers as the students steady themselves and start making their initial, stumpy cylinders. Paige visits each of their stations, giving directions on how to carry out their next movements. When she stops in front of Marlee's station, Paige admires her concentration and steady hand but says nothing at first. Her gaze is fixed on Marlee's slip-covered hands molding the clay upwards with a touch that is both careful and firm.

"I'm not sure I'm doing this right," Marlee says, bringing Paige's attention back to the moment. "Can you help?"

Paige leans over Marlee's wheel, assessing the distance between her two hands and how they guide the clay.

"Could you maybe help me position my hands the right way?"

Paige is reticent but nods. She stands behind Marlee, placing her hands around Marlee's. Coconut wafts from Marlee's hair—a nice break from the moldy-earth aromas that fill the room. With her chest against Marlee's back, she is suddenly aware of how awkwardly she's breathing. Paige likes to maintain a slow, steady breath when throwing on the wheel but instead her pace is quick and shallow when she isn't holding it in all together.

"Get the wheel going," Paige says. Her voice is low. Once the wheel is at a steady pace, Paige places their hands on either side of the clay.

Ned interrupts. "Are you guys reenacting *Ghost?*" He chuckles, pleased with his unoriginal joke that Paige hears every time she guides someone when they're throwing.

Paige looks at him for a second but does not answer. She shifts her focus back to Marlee's misshapen cylinder. "Use your thumbs as a guide for space during the first pull." Paige weaves her thumbs under Marlee's. Slip envelopes their hands together like a plaster cast. "Now anchor your elbows like you did when you were centering and pull up."

Marlee's shoulders tense beneath Paige's chest. Marlee pulls the walls three times like Paige did. She turns her head and smiles. Paige can feel her instinct to jump back, like a stunt rope from a movie is yanking her back.

Paige rinses her hands in the bucket at the front of Marlee's wheel but does not make eye contact while she asks if anyone has any questions. From the corner of her eye she can see all the cylinders wobble, but no one objects or asks for attention. "I'm just going to go out for a smoke and then I'll be back in."

The metal door creaks open, echoing in the warehouse studio behind her. In the distance, cars speed over the hot asphalt and honk with impatience—fighting for attention. Paige doesn't smoke but she can't think of a good reason to excuse herself from the class. In the unusual summer heat, clay dries to her hands. She wipes the dust on her pants, but she can still feel heat that is not her own.

Paige rejoins her students. They sit idle at their wheels, unsure of the next step. Paige's cheeks flush as she wonders whether they will notice she doesn't smell like cigarettes. She sits down at her wheel and shows them the malleability of the clay. Her fingers guide her cylinder into a bowl then a plate then back to a cylinder.

"You're welcome to make whatever you want, but know that mistakes can always be fixed." She smiles.

Marlee smiles back.

•

"I CAN EAT," Paige says.

The server leads them to their table—a small two-top with a bench on one side and a chair on the other. Paige assumes her seat on the bench, thankful that there is no opportunity to sit next to one another. On the flip side, she now has to endure prolonged periods of eye contact.

"I don't mean to make you nervous," Marlee says.

Paige wants to say she isn't, but she's adjusted her napkin and silverware and seat too many times for it to be anything other than nerves.

Paige shakes her head. "I just haven't done this in a while." She takes a sip of her drink. "Actually, I've never done this per se."

"Date?"

"Well, I dated several years ago."

"But never a woman."

"Not until now." Paige tries to read Marlee's reaction, but her face is neutral. *Hazard of the job*, Paige thinks.

•

PAIGE TENDS HER STUDENTS' WORK between the first and second classes. She marvels at Marlee's output—leaving the first class having finished a bowl and two vases. All three had a lean and uneven structure, but Paige admires her tenacity. Ned and the Jacksons had managed to complete one wobbly cylinder apiece. Nothing she can't work with. Paige loosens the bags around each piece, releasing a smell of mold and dirt into the studio in exchange for fresh air to dry out the clay walls—still malleable but firm enough to trim during the second class. When they reach the ideal dryness, Paige places a damp piece of paper towel at the bottom of the plastic bag and seals it around the vessel once more.

Paige arrives at the studio with makeup on that she hasn't worn since her third wedding anniversary, two years ago. She can't remember how old it is. If makeup can go bad it probably did, but it didn't have a funny smell, so Paige used it all the same.

Five minutes after class is supposed to start, only Marlee and Ned are sitting at their wheels. For the most part, people don't have trouble remembering that she runs two classes the first week, but every once in a while people forget and come back for the third class realizing their mistake. Over the years she's gotten complaints about her class structure, but it is easier to manage space and the structural integrity of the clay if classes are close together.

Paige looks at Marlee and Ned. "Let's get started." Paige stifles a sigh. It doesn't bother her that the Jacksons aren't present. It's their money. But there is no avoiding Marlee without risking unprofessionalism. She can't favor Ned the entire time and leave Marlee to figure it out.

All three walk over to the shelves where their work is wrapped beneath plastic bags. Paige pulls out a mug and a vase of her own. "I let these pieces dry a little differently so you can see the difference in moisture levels with various stages of drying."

The first piece is still wet, as if it were just thrown. "This was tied up in a plastic bag for three days without being exposed to any air," Paige says. She touches her fingers to the side of the cylinder, leaving fingerprint ridges in the clay. "Yours have been opened periodically over the last few days to let them get to the leather-hard state."

With Marlee's permission, Paige unwraps one of her cylinders and touches the walls. Her fingerprints are faint—unnoticeable to an unconcentrated eye.

The last one is bone-dry, lacking any moisture and can't be worked on any further. Paige breaks off a piece of the rim. Dust and flakes fall into the base of the piece. She dumps the brittle cylinder into a barrel of recycled clay. The dry piece soaks up water as it sinks into the sediment.

"Today we're going to flip our pots and trim them." Paige flips her pot over and places it in the perceived middle of the wheel. Going slow, Paige eyes the wobble and gives her vessel a few love taps until the wobble disappears. Centered. Fresh clay is ripped and then rolled into four equal balls and pressed evenly around the pot, securing it to the wheel. The wheel spins below the sharp steel trimming knife Paige wields as she presses into the center of the pot. Clay ribbons fall down the side and spin into the basin. When she's done, the bottom is nearly hollow. Just a thin layer of clay between her fingers and the inside of the pot. A smooth rim balances the piece on the table.

She stops the wheel and Marlee stands up straight. Ned still stands by his wheel, unmoved through the whole demonstration.

"All right," Paige says. "Let's give this a shot."

Ned and Marlee each pick their first piece to work on and start to center them on the wheel. Ned, a little heavy handed, taps too hard the first few times, making his piece jump a bit on the wheel. He grimaces and tries to push his pot to the center with a more subtle touch. After almost knocking it over, he finally asks Paige for help.

Paige kneels down next to Ned's wheel and gets him to lower his speed just slightly. Tap. Tap. Tap. She coaxes it into place.

A skipping sound is coming from Marlee's wheel. "Paige, do you think you can help me center mine as well?"

Paige is slow to stand up but nods. Tap. Tap. Tap.

"You can go ahead and secure it to the wheel now," Paige says.

"Thanks for your help."

"Happy to." Paige stands up and goes to check on Ned.

"Paige?"

She turns to face Marlee.

"Would you like to get drinks tomorrow night?"

Paige's face feels hot. She imagines she looks like a cherry against the dust and white of the clay around her.

"Smooth," Ned says.

Marlee doesn't acknowledge him.

Paige fumbles with her words, trying to keep a professional front. "Why don't we talk after class," she says.

Marlee smiles at her and goes back to trimming her work.

For the rest of the class, Paige stays at her wheel or squarely between Marlee and Ned, not favoring either of them. When they're done with the wheels, she moves them to tables where they can add, remove, or displace clay until they feel their vessel is whole and complete. Stamps, carving tools, colored slip—everything is at their disposal, keeping everyone occupied.

Before class is over, Paige asks that they both etch their names into the bottom of their pieces. "They'll have gone through the first firing by the next class so you can glaze them and start on your next pieces."

Ned nods and leaves.

Marlee lingers by the door of the studio, spinning a card between her thumb and index finger. "I'm going to be at this bar tomorrow night at seven. I'd love to see you there." She passes the card to Paige. "I know it's last minute so if you can't make it, just give me a call."

Marlee's writing loops together in a print-cursive hybrid. Close and direct all at once. Marlee places her hand on Paige's and gives a gentle squeeze. "I hope you decide to join me."

Paige stays put as the door closes behind Marlee.

•

"LET'S MAKE SOME DINNER DECISIONS before we start trading life stories," Marlee says. Her smile is kind and genuine, even in the dim light.

Paige takes her time deciding. She doesn't want to be obvious and order the cheapest thing on the menu, though she imagines the mushroom soup would be quite good. She opts for the grilled chicken and vegetables—a tolerable compromise between her stomach and her wallet. Marlee orders the seabass.

Marlee sips the last of her gin and tonic with patience.

"My last first date was seven years ago." Paige can feel the compass in her mind spinning, unsure of the right thing to say. She sips her cider to buy some time, but the needle does not point to anything. She picks a detail at random. "Our divorce was finalized a year ago and I haven't dated since."

"Of course, there's plenty that happened between your first date with your ex-husband and your divorce."

"A marriage, I guess."

She thinks about their first dates, back when they made time for each other. The days that passed by when they didn't see each other without either of them noticing, or at least not mentioning it. The days when they fought. The days when they didn't fight were the ones that left a pit in her stomach. Paige gets the same pit when she thinks about those days now.

Paige doesn't like talking about her ex, but as she replays the memories in her head, she finds herself wanting to share some of it with Marlee. Some days it feels like a black spot in her past, and other days it doesn't feel like it happened at all. "We probably got married too young. He served me divorce papers because he thought I worked too much." He worked just as much at his dad's law firm.

"What made you decide to join me for drinks?"

Paige pushes food around on her plate before she looks at Marlee. Paige's ex-husband's words eat at her. She enjoys working in the studio, but she doesn't like idea of not seeing Marlee because of it. A trade-off that had not existed in the confines of her marriage. Her marriage had kept its shape from their early days, small changes left unnoticed. Many days apart and too few days together in-between turned separation into resentment into separation. "Because I wanted to have drinks with you." Her words as true as saying I don't know.

Marlee smiles before she tells of her unmarried past. Paige feels the muscles of her core engage as she leans in while Marlee talks. A smile creeps across her face as Marlee tells her about her time in the Peace Corps before getting her degrees to be a practicing psychologist. When she tries to down-play her achievements, Paige's heart softens knowing that she has something else in common with Marlee.

The waiter asks if they want the dessert menu. Marlee's eyes light up as much as her smile. "Besides the drinks, it's the best part of dinner."

Paige agrees to the spontaneous last course and opts for a cup of black coffee. Marlee orders the cheesecake and talks of her work as they wait.

"I prefer to work with families, though they can be the most heart-breaking. Too often I see parents put their children through the wringer trying to deal with their own baggage. But if I can help them—if they start going to therapy early enough—it can be extremely rewarding."

"Sounds like you take your work home with you."

"I try not to but it's sometimes unavoidable. No matter how much they teach you to keep your distance and not get invested, I'm still human. I don't like to see people hurting."

Marlee's empathy nestles into Paige's heart.

Before the bill hits the table, Marlee intercepts it from the server.

"Please, at least let me split it with you."

"Not a chance," Marlee says. "I asked you out."

Paige gives Marlee a quiet thank you. She worries that she is a cheap date, though she never really understood the negative connotations to that identity.

Outside the doors of the restaurant, Paige and Marlee stand closer than friends do—but not as close as lovers.

"I had a nice night," Paige offers.

"That makes me happy to hear. If nothing else, you'll have a positive story to tell about your first date with a woman," Marlee says with a wink.

Paige blushes.

Marlee is gentle when she wraps her arms around Paige in a full hug but does not ask or try for a kiss. Marlee disappears into a sea of people. Cars whir past pushing the air around Paige. Her skin tingles.

·

MARLEE AND NED ARE THE FIRST to show up for the third and final class. The other two students are not far behind them. Like Paige had expected, the Jacksons were confused about the class dates.

"Not to fret. We'll get you guys caught up." She ushers everyone over to the glazing station. "Since everyone will have to do this at some point, I'll explain glazing first and then we'll take the two of you back to discuss trimming."

Hanging from a peg board are patterned clay titles covered in various colors of glaze. Some are glossy while others look like they could be velvet. While they put the finishing aesthetic touches on a piece, they are also a crucial step to sealing the clay.

"When pots go in for their glaze firing, the glaze compound melts and bonds to the clay creating a glass-like seal, making the piece waterproof." Paige puts out several examples of her own work to show what a successful glaze firing looks like, along with a few pieces that were forever ruined. "It's important to be careful when applying the glaze. Too much will cause the glaze to run onto the kiln shelves, ruining a shelf and your pot." Shards of kiln shelves stick to the feet of pots, rendering them rough and unusable. Paige shows them how to use wax to prevent glaze from sticking where it shouldn't.

Paige leaves Marlee and Ned to choose glazes and talk while she takes the Jacksons over to the wheels to demonstrate trimming. Even over the snide remarks between Mr. and Mrs. Jackson, Paige hears Ned trying to pry information from Marlee.

"How was the date?" Ned jabs his elbow at Marlee's arm like they're buddies. Paige's heart rate increases.

"What date?" Marlee is coy and subtle. The Jacksons do not notice. Ned doesn't look to Paige for denial or confirmation. Class goes on.

Paige oscillates between the two pair—making sure everyone has enough guidance but also enough space to be creative. Even when she's not working with Marlee, her words create the sweetest white noise. From the corner of her eye, Paige watches Marlee move around the studio without fear. Her presence cuts through the tension of the Jacksons, and through Ned's unending questioning about Marlee's personal life. Marlee doesn't seem phased by any of it.

Envy rises in Paige. She wishes she could walk through a room without worrying about someone else's unspoken opinions about her, and without judging her own creativity or craft.

Three hours ends faster than everyone expects. Paige invites the Jacksons to glaze their pieces at a later date. They accept and argue about the missed class on the way to their high-end, eco-friendly sedan. Ned lingers for a bit, posturing that he might actually sign up for the full course next time. Paige says she hopes he does but knows he likely won't and she'll only see him once more when he picks up his fired pot the following week.

Paige and Marlee stand alone in the studio shop, but do not speak for a few moments. The silence is warm and comforting, instead of awkward like Paige is used to with anyone else. Paige walks towards Marlee. She lets her fingers search for Marlee's until they touch and tangle together. ∎

Dear Reader,

When was the last time you felt uncentered?

Shanda Connolly

New Moon in Aries

So who the hell were those men who told us we were nothing? Why did we let them take us so far adrift from ourselves, into those dark, dangerous places that we had to fight so hard and long to swim back from? Our mothers didn't know to warn us, I guess. But now, a half century later, we know better. We vow that we'll teach our daughters.

With a new moon in Aries, we head to the water to give thanks for the joy and peace we've found and ask for some more. The sand and air, perfect, not too hot, not too cold: spring is finally here, a time for new beginnings. The ocean, resplendent, encompassing the infinite horizon on the edge of Venice and Santa Monica. All of its power right at our toes.

We sit in ritual silence, then wade back through the sand to the rows of pricey homes, where pretty people play music, drink, and eat. A man wearing sunglasses standing near a barbeque calls out to me and offers a cocktail sausage. No thanks, I say, I'm a vegetarian now.

Lydia McDermott

Big Muffet

was on a diet. She took her lunch of lowfat cottage cheese outside on a stool so she didn't have to watch the others eating hamburgers and pizza. She mixed in pears to spice it up a little and proceeded to savor each little curd, hoping it would fill her if she took her time. Then (wouldn't you know it?), along came a big, nasty spider.

Muffet breathed deep—she was not going to run. She looked at the hairy thing, stared it down, ignored the gut instinct that told her to get the hell out of there. But spiders have too many eyes and that damn spider crawled right under Muffet and took a juicy bite out of a little cheek. Muffet jumped, screamed, ran— typical. Next day, she woke up big and muscular—body-builder muscular—and she had kind of (you guessed it) a sixth spider sense. She was quick, limber and hella strong.

Now Big Muffet eats steak rare, licks the blood off the plate. Fuck curds and whey. She's big and powerful and hungry.

Courtney Bambrick

Instructions for Needles and Pins

Create a fist out of your hand,
flatten out the palm,
squeeze back into a fist again.

Imagine the blood moving
molasses through your veins,
around cartilage of knuckles,
the fine bones of your fingers.

Press your hands together
now, as if in prayer, but
press hard,
an angry prayer—rub
your hands against one another,

drag skin against skin until
it is hot—until your flesh
buzzes, until the burn
turns back on itself, and
subsides.

        Or let the pricking
numb your whole hand, arm,
body. Let sensation become
your complete, electrified self.

Harper Walton

Daisies

You're six and you've forgotten your PE kit. You know what this means. Everyone does. You must do the class wearing your vest and no trousers. Just your small white briefs. Looking around the sports hall at thirty other kids in their shorts and trainers, you feel like _______. Everyone's looking at you. Some seem sympathetic, having gone through this before. Some are trying not to laugh. You want to _______. Staring up at your PE teacher, a woman in her fifties, you feel nothing but _______. You look down at your pale slim hairless legs, the bulge in your pants from your little penis. Your vest isn't long enough to cover it. This moment _______ you. A sharp whistle begins the class. You jog around the edges of the echoing hall, _______ your body.

You're ten and you've forgotten your knee-high socks for the school football tournament. A nice quiet girl called Imogen offers you her spare socks. She holds them out to you: small, pastel pink, frilly hem, with an embroidered daisy on each ankle. I can't wear those, you immediately think. But you're desperate to play in the tournament. You play football every break and lunch, and the boys have given you the reputation of a lazy goal-hanger. It's time to prove them wrong. You hold Imogen's socks in a tightly balled fist. "Thanks," you say. She looks _______. In the changing room, you peel off your plain black school socks. You slowly pull on Imogen's. Looking down, your feet are now indistinguishable from a girl's. Your heart _______. Your mind is _______. You've never felt so _______ before. You squeeze into your Nike T90 boots, the ones that Wayne Rooney wears. The daisies and the frills poke out the top like weeds through cement. You make a promise to yourself: _I'll play so well today, no one will notice what socks I'm wearing._ You sprint out onto the dewy field and transform into an absolute _______.

originally published by the Young Poets Network
as a winner of the Here and Now challenge, 2024

Be Guāi-et

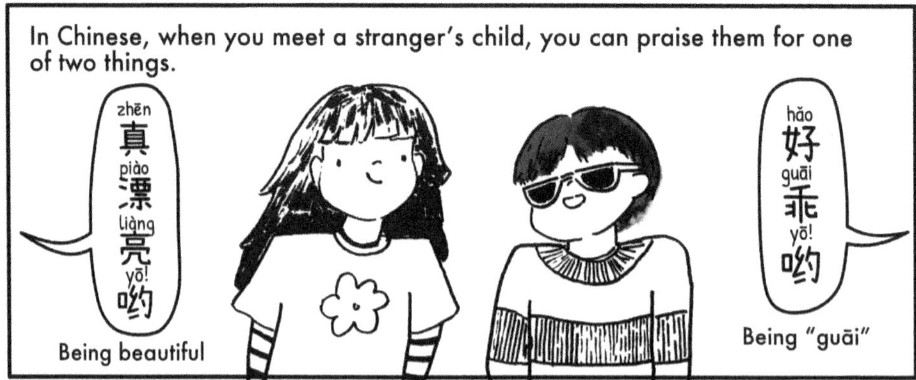
In Chinese, when you meet a stranger's child, you can praise them for one of two things.
zhēn
真
piào
漂
liàng
亮
yō!
哟
Being beautiful
hǎo
好
guāi
乖
yō!
哟
Being "guāi"

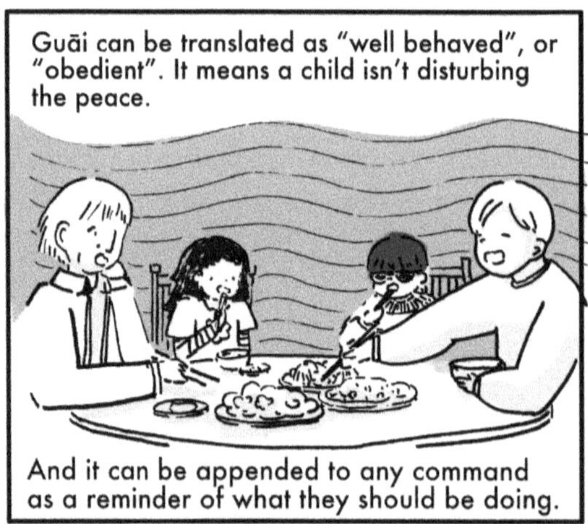
Guāi can be translated as "well behaved", or "obedient". It means a child isn't disturbing the peace.
And it can be appended to any command as a reminder of what they should be doing.

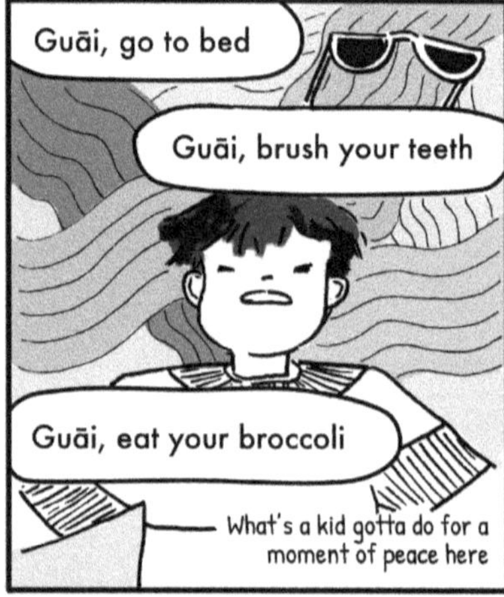
Guāi, go to bed
Guāi, brush your teeth
Guāi, eat your broccoli
What's a kid gotta do for a moment of peace here

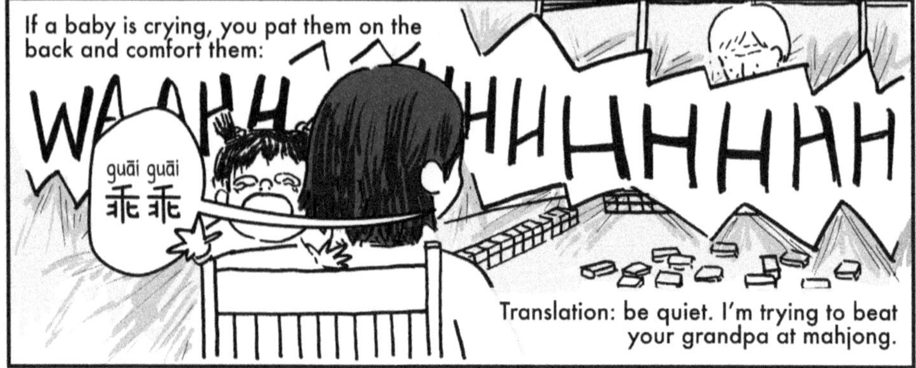
If a baby is crying, you pat them on the back and comfort them:
WAAHHHHHHHHHH
guāi guāi
乖乖
Translation: be quiet. I'm trying to beat your grandpa at mahjong.

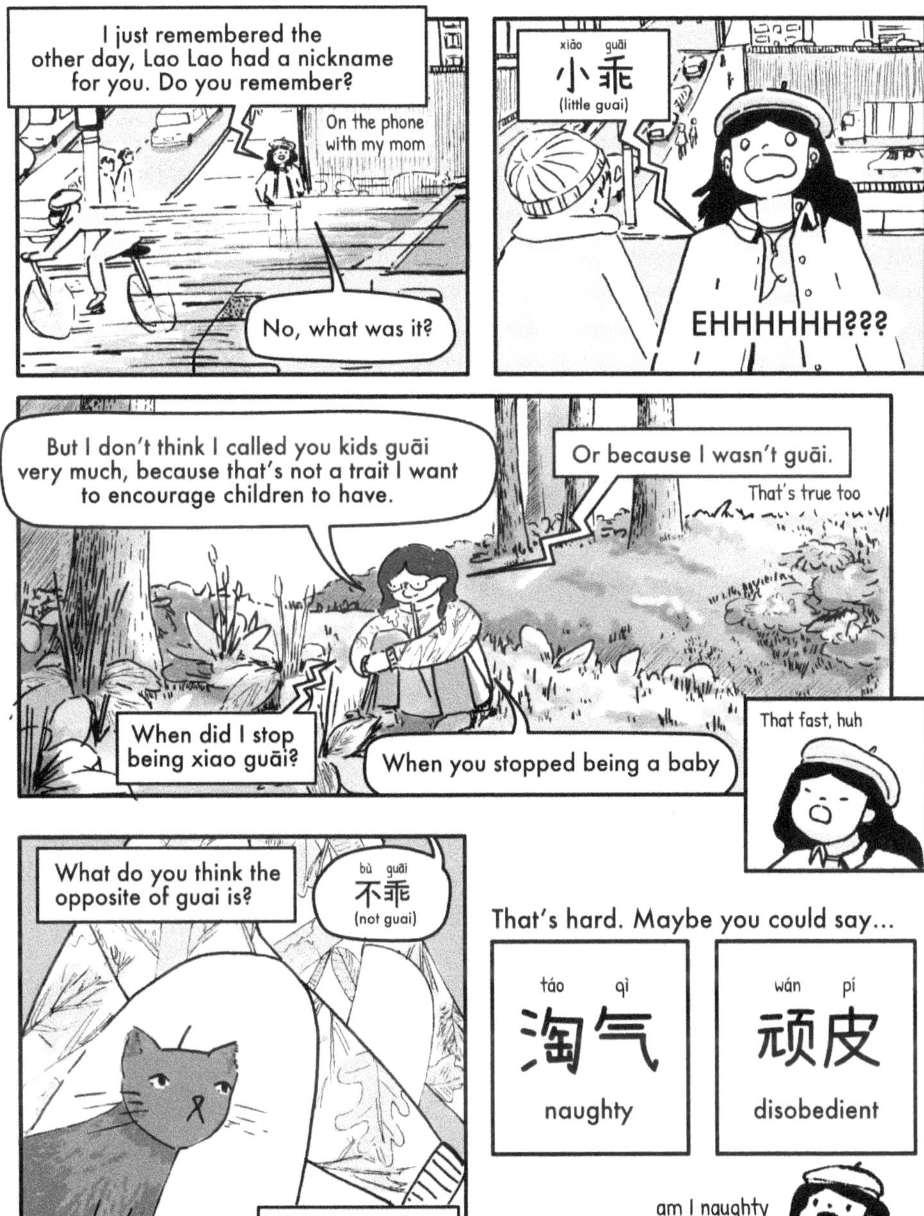
I just remembered the other day, Lao Lao had a nickname for you. Do you remember?
On the phone with my mom
No, what was it?
xiāo guāi
小乖
(little guai)
EHHHHHH???
But I don't think I called you kids guāi very much, because that's not a trait I want to encourage children to have.
Or because I wasn't guāi.
That's true too
When did I stop being xiao guāi?
When you stopped being a baby
That fast, huh
What do you think the opposite of guai is?
bù guāi
不乖
(not guai)
That's hard. Maybe you could say...
táo qì
淘气
naughty
wán pí
顽皮
disobedient
am I naughty
Other than that

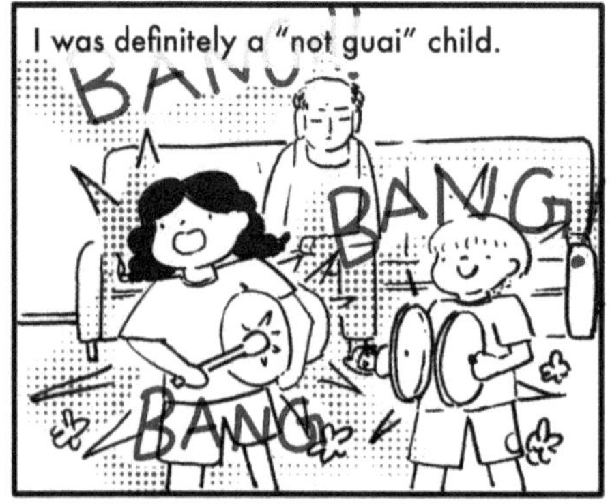

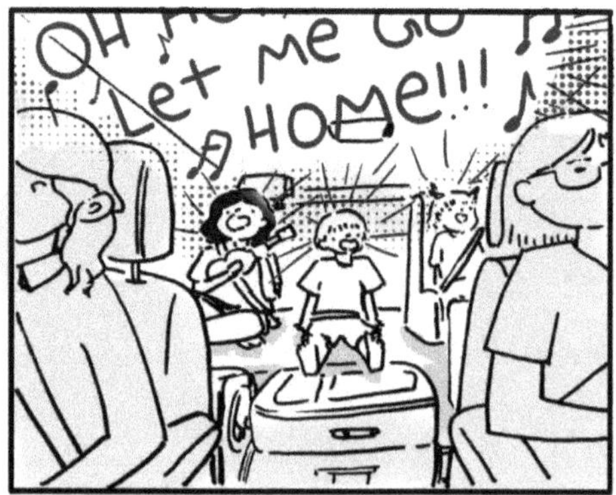

But I think that's because I have not guāi parents!

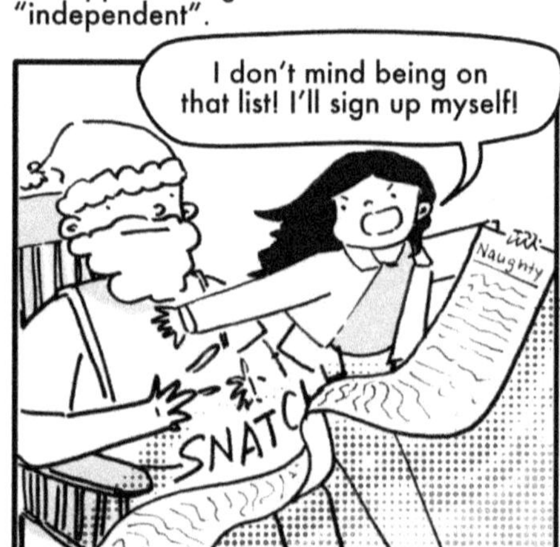

And in America, people teach their kids to question rules and the person in charge.

The opposite of guai should be "independent".

I am a product of my upbringing. And my upbringing was…

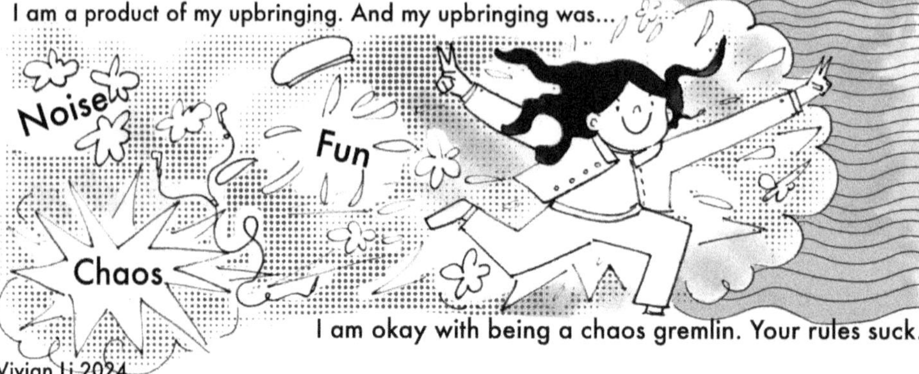

Erin Armstrong

The Wrestling Match

There's a faint sound
of a car or two driving
down the street;
it's too early to see
the clouds blanket the sun;
too early to hear the Steller's jays.

This used to be
my quiet

now interrupted.

My daughter runs
toward me demanding
her morning songs.

Pine needles scatter as she reaches
for an ugly ornament off the Christmas tree
—a small stuffed penguin
with a cherry red Santa hat.

I thought I'd put the ornaments out
of her reach but today her arms
are longer, so she runs off.
My voice echoes off the fireplace:
bring it back!

The routine of our morning
now interrupted by a Christmas
tree and its trimmings.

I have not needed an alarm
in nineteen months
because my daughter cries instead.
First, an irrepressible whine,
then tears. Now she can
yell *MOMMY!*

Each morning, I remove
dead weight from the crib—
this daughter of mine who
does not want to part with her
pacifier or stuffed animals, yet
calls for me at five-thirty
insisting it's time.

I am a green wrestler:
inexperienced mother,
second-guessing my takedowns,
my footwork,
the ring I am in.

This girl of mine goes stiff
when she doesn't want
to be moved.
She transforms her twenty-six pounds
into forty-six.

I move her from
room to room; extract her
from her tantrum in the corner;
bearhug her and plop
her down; I insist
she put away her books,
the toys scattered in the hall.

When she wiggles and tries
to scramble out of my arms,
I keep her pressed to the floor.
She reaches for what I've asked,
puts away the last silver piece
to a game she doesn't play.

Every day, as the sun sets,
I sing her a song, shut her
door, hear the rain of her
sound machine ring off her walls
and feel like she's had the clean finish.

Michelle Herman

Sea-Change

WHEN SHE WAS TWO AND A HALF, and I was on sabbatical from teaching—and from Ohio, where we lived, where I felt I was in exile—I took my daughter to a children's production of *A Midsummer Night's Dream*. We were living in New York City then, just for that year: the place I still thought of as my "real home"—or, as I taught my child to say, her "ancestral home." It was the sort of phrase we'd pull out to dazzle people (yes, I know how obnoxious that is; somehow I did not know it then) with the wit and wisdom of my tiny daughter. Grace was small for her age, too, so people were especially amazed—shocked—when she said the things she said. When she recited "The Owl and the Pussy-Cat" in its entirety, or politely asked a waiter for *water in a wine glass, please*. It seemed to me that both of us enjoyed this. It is entirely possible that this attention from strangers and acquaintances was what started her on a path toward a career in theater, even before she saw her first play.

That year of my sabbatical, we were bartering my husband's skills in exchange for a rent-free apartment that needed remodeling in Brooklyn Heights. Mornings, while I wrote, Grace and her father made drawings and paintings together or built complicated block structures in the living room of our construction-zone apartment. In the afternoon, after I'd rejoined the two of them for lunch, sometimes all three of us ventured out together to a museum or one of the many playgrounds of Central Park before Glen headed for the studio that was his for the year in Tribeca; sometimes Grace and I would have our own adventures in the city and Glen would go straight to work. Either way, eventually she and I would return to the apartment— her father rarely left the studio before midnight—and play let's pretend for hours before bedtime. *Let's be orphans*, she would say. Or, *let's be sisters who are teenagers*. Or, *I'm the bunny and you're the girl who finds the bunny in the woods.*

Let's be best friends. Let's be farmers and it's time to pick the vegetables and take them to market. Let's play I'm the mama, you're the baby.

We were characters from her favorite books, the ones I read to her at bedtime—the friends-for-life Betsy and Tacy from the series both of us loved most, or two sisters from *The Five Little Peppers and How They Grew* or *All-of-A-Kind Family*. We were enchanted creatures in a forest. We were lost at sea.

•

IT'S BEEN TWENTY-EIGHT YEARS since my New York sabbatical. I have now lived in Ohio for longer than New York, even when I take into account that bonus year, years later. I first left the city—that's what I called it growing up, and it's what I can't help calling it still, just *the city*, as if there weren't any other—when I was twenty-nine, intending to return after I had finished graduate school in Iowa (Iowa! A place I could not have located on a map). Instead I moved farther west for two years, then landed in Ohio, where I found a job and finally gave up subletting my sublet in *the city*.

I'm in my thirty-sixth year in Ohio. The first three decades of my life seem so much longer in my memory than these last three and a half. The years of my daughter's childhood, for instance, seem to have flashed by; the years of my own childhood took forever.

This is a not uncommon way of processing one's memories, I understand. But that doesn't make it any less astonishing to me. Just as the knowledge that everyone is surprised by their own aging doesn't make my own more palatable. My grandmother, with whom I was closer than anyone until my daughter came along, used to say, *Inside I feel the same. And no one knows! No one knows I'm just the same.* I was sixteen, eighteen, twenty, but I thought I understood—I was able to project myself into my own future and think: *I'm going to feel the same way.*

And I do. I look in the mirror and see the sixty-nine-year-old version of the permanent me. The one who inside feels "the same." I never thought to ask my grandmother how old she felt—how old her true self was. My own is forty-one, when Grace was a toddler. Those miserable teens and twenties, those fraught thirties, are behind the permanent me, the one who has found herself.

That this self resides in Columbus, Ohio, seemed for a long time like a cosmic joke. But the sixty-nine-year-old version of myself has made peace with it at last. These last few years, I have even been enjoying it.

One reason for this peace, no doubt, is that the time to leave is near, or near-ish. I've stayed here all these years despite my multiple complaints about it—which boiled down to one big complaint, that Columbus had too many of the disadvantages of a real city without the many advantages (a complaint that neatly covered such matters as traffic, parking, noise, and crime, as well as the absence of good public transportation, theater and museums, and, I always claimed, interesting people)—because of my job.

But now I am retired from teaching, and sometime in the next few years, I'll leave Columbus. Where I'll go depends on Grace. Which is ironic, I suppose. Finally free, for the first time in my life, to choose where I want to live, I cede the choice to her. Because I want to be the sort of grandmother to her children, when she has them, that mine was to me.

And chances are that Grace will be in, or near, *the city*. It's where she has lived for years now. It's the place she set her course for as soon as she was able. That's my doing, I know. I taught her that it was home, our *real* home. Now she can't imagine wanting to live anywhere else. She calls Columbus "the place where my parents live."

•

Five years ago:

It is after midnight when I finally take a break from dancing at my sixty-fourth birthday party to sit for just a minute on the couch beside my husband, who doesn't dance—who has never danced. Glen is a Southern Baptist preacher's son, an introvert, paralyzingly self-conscious in social situations (so I do my best not to put him in them very often—but this, of course, is a special occasion: my will-you-still-need-me/will-you-still-feed-me birthday). Me, I'm a Brooklyn-born Jew, an extrovert who craves connection to other people, who hasn't a self-conscious bone in her body. We're an odd couple who get along the way only people who are completely mismatched can. Which is to say: we let each other be, and be who we are, even when we're mystified by the form that being takes. Like now.

Are you having fun? he asks. The answer is obvious. I am surrounded by people I love. We are dancing to a mix of Beyoncé and the Isley Brothers and Prince and Talking Heads and Celia Cruz and I'd asked my friends to please bring food and needs, so there is plenty of wonderful food, sweet rice cakes and crispy tofu and macaroni and cheese and cookies and pâté and bread (they have mostly neglected to bring needs). I shrug and smile. I know what he really means is: Can you explain *why* is this fun?

I can't answer that—that would be a matter of explaining why I am who I am. We've both tried over the many years of our marriage, lots of times, to explain ourselves to each other. It's possible that we've gotten along as well as we have because this question is still interesting to both of us and also because it's unanswerable. And I'd give it another shot right now, but the next song on my party playlist has come on, and it's Celia Cruz's "La Vida Es Un Carnaval," one of my favorites, so I'm up on my feet again even as Glen is saying, *But you didn't even know any of these people a year ago.*

He's exaggerating—it's been more like a year and a half—but I know what he means by this, too. My life has changed completely over the last year and a half. The party is full of people I've met in the ballet classes I take every day.

And this is the other reason I am at peace with—that I have found joy in—my life in Columbus after all these years. I have fallen in with a crowd of other late-to-ballet dancers, people whom I never would have met if not for the dance classes that we take together.

Two of my new friends are my dance teachers, Russ and Fili. Eighteen of them are other serious amateur dancers who are going to be onstage with me in a few weeks in an experimental dance and theater piece we've been rehearsing for months.

All of this is puzzling to Glen. I can't blame him. It surprises me too.

•

Back in Ohio after the sabbatical year, a children's cartoon-style biography of Jackson Pollock became one of three-year-old Grace's favorite books—we read it every night at bedtime. There was a panel on one page that showed Lee Krasner, Pollock's wife, demanding to know what Jackson had done with her eggbeater—and, in the next panel, there he is bent over a canvas, using an eggbeater to fling paint.

When Grace asked, one morning, for my eggbeater, I didn't have to ask her why. Her father and I covered the playroom floor with taped-together vinyl tablecloths, and for many days over many weeks, she splashed and splattered and egg-beat and dripped paint on large sheets of posterboard we taped to the vinyl. *I'm Jackson Pollock*, she told us. *I am not me, okay?*

·

A Midsummer Night's Dream was the first play she ever saw. She had been listening to music—Hendrix, punk, the Grateful Dead, jazz, heavy metal, Hip-Hop, and R&B—since she was in utero, and looking at paintings since the day she was born (when Glen held her up to one and said, *Look at this, Grace Jane. This is called a **landscape***). On hot days, that first summer of her life, I'd strap her into a front-facing pack and walk laps through the chilly galleries of the Columbus Art Museum. And that year we lived in the city, we spent so much time at the Metropolitan Museum that she nicknamed all the abstract paintings in the Lila Acheson Wallace Wing, and if her father and I lingered too long elsewhere—looking at seventeenth century Dutch still lifes or Quattrocento paintings—Grace would cry, *Get me back to the twentieth century!*

And she was the daughter of a writer, so books were as much a part of her life as breakfast and bath time.

Now here was theater, which was altogether new to her.

We sat side by side on a hard bench watching simplified complications ensue in an adumbration of a forest. I kept a careful eye on her for signs that we should bolt—at any moment, I feared, she might scream, *Get me back to real life!* But she was silent and attentive. And then Puck cast his spell and Bottom's head was swallowed by a papier-mâché ass's head and my daughter gasped and stood up on the bench and grabbed me, one hand on my shoulder, the other grasping my hair—and when Titania began to stir, she shouted, *Oh NO! She's going to fall in love with a DONKEY!*

She was laughing and crying at the same time. *I can't believe it*, she said. *Mama, I just can't believe it.*

This wasn't what she meant, I knew. She meant, *I believe it.* She meant she was amazed because she did.

•

I TOOK MY FIRST BALLET CLASS at the age of sixty-two because I couldn't think of a good reason not to. The dance studio that had just opened was only steps from my house: how lazy would I have to be not to try a class? I remembered that I'd joked—half joked; what I'd thought was a joke—when Grace was four, taking classes at the ballet school downtown, that they should offer simultaneous ballet classes for the parents who were sitting around waiting for the children to get out of class. We all brought books, or work—or knitting or a crossword puzzle—but what we actually did to pass the time was talk. It was all right. It was nice, in fact. I didn't mind chatting with the other mothers (it was always mothers, then). I spent a lot of time in those years talking to other mothers while our children danced or sang in choir or took a music lesson or auditioned for a play. I spent so much time (we all spent so much time) waiting around. So we talked. We compared notes. Sometimes we told each other secrets. We saw each other only while we sat and waited, once a week, so it felt safe.

It's only now that it has dawned on me that this was something like group therapy, that we all needed badly to talk to people we didn't really know about our kids and our marriages. About things that worried us, that scared us. About what it felt like to be always waiting.

•

By spring of my first year of dancing, I'd signed on for a performance project, even though the prospect scared me. I'd asked Grace what she thought, whether I should do it. She said, *You'd be surprised by how much working toward a performance motivates you.*

We were on the phone, of course—she was in the city; I was in Columbus—and I said, *That means yes, I should?*

Yes, Mama, she said. *That means you should.*

And so, less than a year after my first ballet class, I was onstage at the Franklinton Playhouse in Columbus, Ohio, where I'd lived so uneasily since 1988. Ten of us, aged twenty-two through seventy-four, danced in a contemporary performance piece that had been made for, made *on*, us.

And I was as hooked now on performance as I was on my daily classes, so that when Russ proposed another, more ambitious project—a full evening of dance and experimental theater—with a longer rehearsal period and twice as many dancers, I was the first to say *yes*, to ask *when do we start?*

•

At Grace's senior thesis show in college, the audience stood, they danced, they shouted. They were laughing and crying at the same time. I was crying too, but not only because of what was happening onstage—a Kabuki dream unfolding, a romance, injustice, villainy and tragedy, the mystery of what was real and what was not—or even only because I was so proud of her. I *missed* her. I missed her already, even though we were, for the moment, in the same room.

I had been missing her for years—she'd just spent four years in college in Connecticut, hundreds of miles from Ohio (and just that past summer she'd been thousands of miles away, in Kyoto)—but soon there would be no pretending anymore that these were sojourns, that she "really" lived with us. Soon, home would be elsewhere—she would be gone for good.

•

I spend a lot of time—too much time, Grace would say—thinking of her. I don't worry about her. Friends ask me that—*is that the trouble, that you're worried?*—but it isn't worry, it's just longing, so sharp it sometimes feel like grief. I miss her company, her conversation.

But it isn't only that. I also miss the child she was. I think about that child, too, so long gone now. I think about Jackson Pollock's eggbeater, I think about that afternoon at *A Midsummer Night's Dream*—I can summon up the memory in such particular detail, that small excited child, her hand on my shoulder, crying out in joy and dread, that it is just as if the scene were unfolding before me now, nearly three decades on.

I think about *let's make up commercials for pretend products and you be Tacy, I'll be Betsy*, and when she "directed" herself and her friend Kristin as they acted out *Black Beauty*—Kristin playing Ginger, Grace playing everyone else, horse and human both—and I think about the time I took her to a stage adaptation of *Charlotte's Web* and afterwards she met the actor who played Charlotte and I saw the wheels turning, saw her *decide*. And about the summer after that, when she was seven, when "Charlotte" became her first acting teacher and introduced her to Kabuki. And two summers after *that*, when she was reintroduced to Shakespeare, when she memorized and then performed her first-ever monologue—Miranda's from *The Tempest*.

•

As it happened, one of the first shows she would devise with the theater company she founded after college was a reinterpretation of *The Tempest*. She was supporting herself then, in those early years of her career in theater, as the part-time nanny of a little girl. Every weekday afternoon and evening it was *let's be fairies in the forest, let's be girls at summer camp, let's pretend this is a restaurant, let's put on a dancing show.* The subway stop nearest to where she lived then was the last stop in Manhattan on the B line—which made its first stop in Brighton Beach, where I was born, where my parents met and married. About halfway between the two was my old subway stop from when I was the age that Grace was then, fresh out of Brooklyn College.

I think about that girl—the one I was—and how much she'd have liked my daughter. If I concentrate, I can make time collapse, I can put the two together—*let's be sisters, let's be friends*—and imagine for a moment what that looks like.

•

THE GIRL I WAS isn't really gone. She is only invisible. The little girl my daughter was is still here too, deep within her. I thought about this for the first time only after I woke up one morning from a dream that had seemed to be about my daughter and the child she cared for in the city: the child, who in the dream was Grace's and my shared responsibility, had wandered off—I feared she was lost for good. But Grace set out to find her, racing up many flights of stairs and forcing her way past crowds, and in the end she did find her, she was safe, and when at last I made my own way through the crowds, I saw that Grace had the child on her lap on a small bench at the top of the last flight of stairs and they were talking quietly.

I woke up thinking—marveling—she knew exactly what to do, and I saw then that the dream was not about Grace and her six-year-old charge, Ruby. I woke up thinking about how the child my daughter was had been entrusted to the woman she'd become—how she was the one who took care of her now.

•

EIGHT YEARS AGO:

It is my sixty-first birthday. I am visiting Grace in New York, and together we go to the Museum of Modern Art to see a Jackson Pollock show.

We linger in front of every painting—they are like old friends we haven't seen in a long time. As we stand together before one of the first of the drip paintings, Grace bends to read its title. I think—how would it be possible for me not to think?—about the year we lived in New York together, the year between her second and third birthdays, when she didn't know or care what titles artists had given to the paintings they'd made, when she'd name them herself—*Boom!* and *Black Angry Storm* and *Red Green White Fog.*

Now she says, *Mama, look.*

The painting we are in front of, it turns out, is called *Full Fathom Five.* It's from *The Tempest.* It is Ariel, invisibly singing:

> *Full fathom five thy father lies;*
> *Of his bones are coral made;*
> *Those are pearls that were his eyes:*
> *Nothing of him that doth fade,*
> *But doth suffer a sea-change*
> *Into something rich and strange.*

We both laugh. She has just begun work on her production of *The Tempest.* We both say, *I can't believe it.* But that isn't what we mean. We do believe it. It is both surprising and inevitable, like the end of any good story—Jackson Pollock and Shakespeare, why not? The way everything manages to come together. ∎

Mikun Oluwayemi

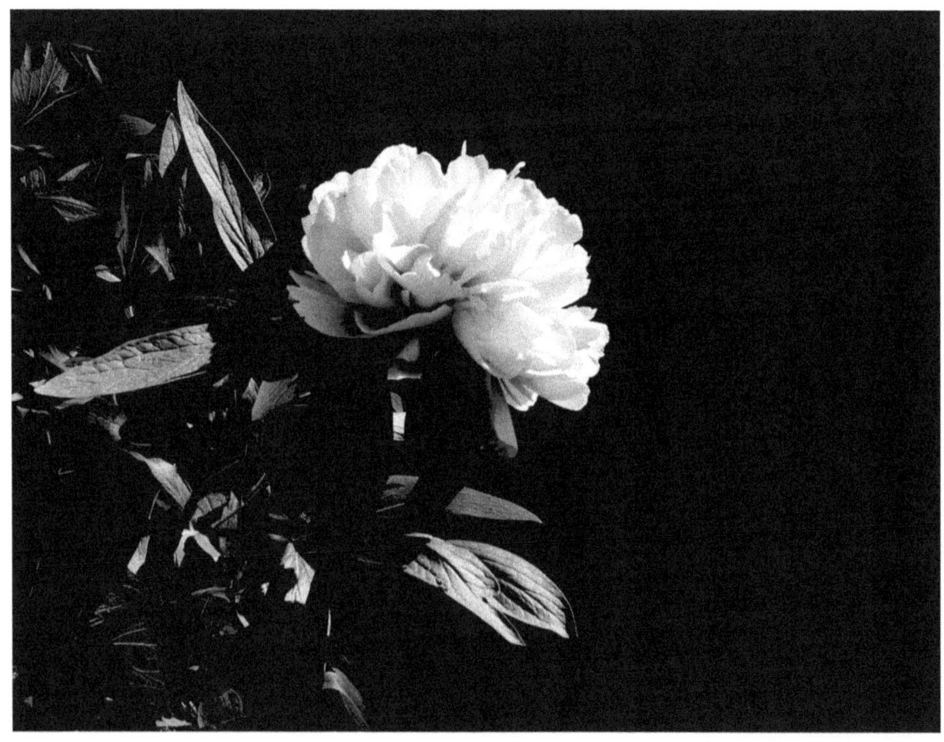

Remember

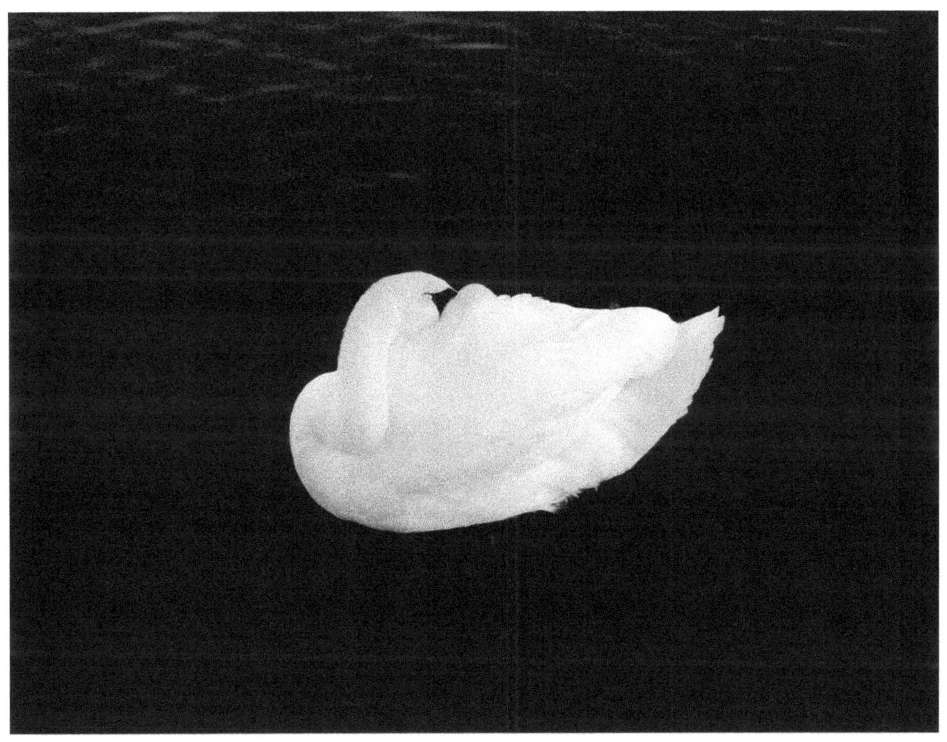

Watch Me

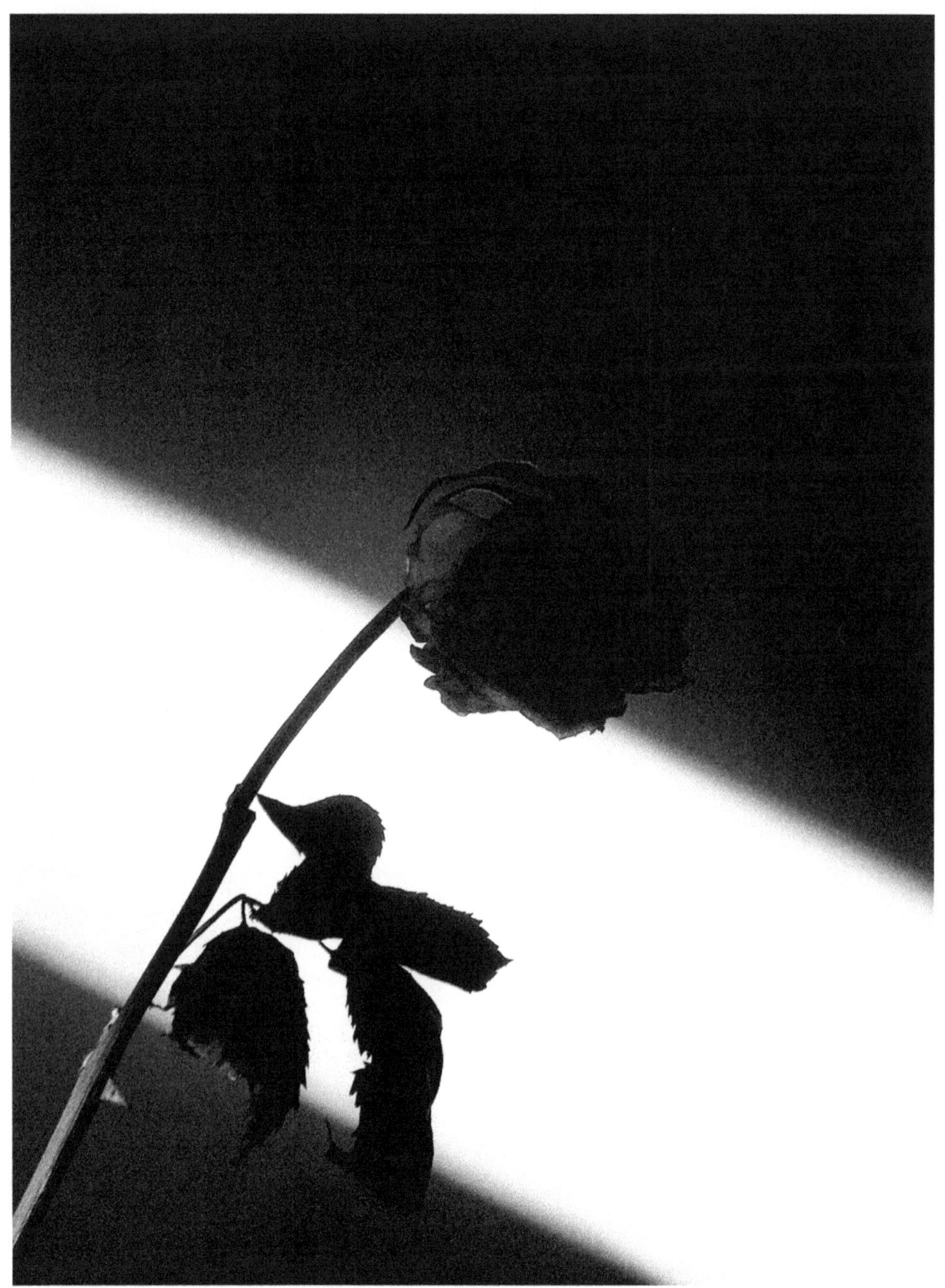

Even Flowers Cast a Black Shadow

Deborah Bacharach

How to Pray

Say anything.
Touch the almost
invisible with calloused
fingertips. That's your skin,
folding like a mud slide. For
seven billion years, sit in the sun,
sit naked in the ocean. In warm breezes
pour on milk and honey. When asked, are you
alright? Lift and lower until your wings align.

Carrie Redway

Father Jupiter

I.

Frankincense hangs in the air. Labradorite sways from my neck. I nod to the ceiling to acknowledge you and

wait several minutes to release my grip on your hand. Place your palm on the blanket so that it does not fall hard. I scan the room for scissors to cut off the hospice bracelet. You wanted it removed all this time.

There is no priest here for cleansing. Your last exhale was purification plenty. I take deep breaths to fill me. We begin again.

I witnessed a beautiful door close while holding my breath under thick and murky water. My enchantment met with weighted sorrow.

I continue to nod my head at nothing.

II.

I watched them tag your feet, shroud your body with a wool blanket, and pull you out of the bed like a hunter might pull a shot deer out of a truck. The funeral worker moved swift. It was nonetheless holy.

I hoped that you had already left this space, and had no concern for any of this. I will hold this scene for you, if you need it.

Jupiter, my thoughts have fizzled to what is right in front of me. And it is your body being carried away.

Tomorrow you will still be dead. The shock will wear thin as vellum. I still want you here

to sniff the same air as I do

to talk while we gather and toss the hedge apples back into the woods that rolled down the hill

to hear the same earthly pulse when ear is to ground.

III.

Lepidolite in my palm, held high to the ceiling.

I remember these things:

Trimming your fingernails. Holding a cool wash cloth to the nape of your neck during a strong bout of dry heaves.

Placing worn loafers on your feet. Whispering, *they are almost here*, when I heard faint ambulance sirens. Seeing a golden glow on you in your bedroom at sunset. Hearing the owl hoot at night

and I became oh so cold.

Jupiter, my thoughts are nocturnal.

Abby E. Murray

Grief in December

It will not be hung on some dumb,
wall-facing branch of the tree.

Mine wants to dazzle on the front,
near the top, like an angel or a star.

No grief is brand new—they're all
heirlooms—and yet, warm light

bounces off my grief like it's been
made of silver fractals forever.

Does that mean grief shines? Mine
likes to think so. It wants to be

brought to parties like champagne,
wants to be passed around like cups

full of bubbles, then it wants
to hammer the temples of anyone

I sat next to or looked at or ate with.
I wish my grief was as unfamiliar

to me as the scent of chimney soot,
or as seasonal as curb-colored, half-

melted snow, but it isn't. It smells
like cinnamon, like peppermint,

like pine: it is evergreen, it is year-
round, swirled into the coat sleeves

and candles of every simple comfort
that tries to obscure it. Every December

grief gets up early and stays up late
with me. I'm telling you, it glows

in the dark, it fills a room. If grief
is the residue of happiness gone

elsewhere, how could it not also
expand as joy does when given

the space it needs? This December
I stop trying to disguise or discard it.

I bring it inside, arrange it like a garland
above the electric fireplace. My friends

admire it when they come over—
they bring their grief too—

and we feel it all, we drink a toast to it,
we garnish our glasses with its barbed leaves.

How Not to Be a Buzzkill at Holiday Gatherings

Multiple sources suggest asking questions
in order to avoid making statements. I'll start.

Can you tell me what you mean by *nice*
or *sober* or *smart* before I take off my coat?

What is the difference between a rocked boat
and a ruffled feather? Do I look like a child?

a chump? a liar? Can I sit here? Is there
anyone with us who believes in the kindness

of pilgrims despite slavery or smallpox or treaties
spun up like lace then torched like greasy rags,

who believes in pie before the possession
of butter or wheat, who pledges allegiance to a flag?

Can anyone fold this napkin into the shape
of a stag? a pumpkin? a rose? Can we talk

about hands that scrub and stir and slice
as well as the ones that don't? Do we hold hands

during prayer to ensure we all burn if one of us
is consumed by flame? What do you mean by *grace*?

Does anyone have something they'd like me to say?
Where is the wine? Red or white? How much?

Where do you keep your salt, your gin, your limes?
Anyone have a song to sing? Another?

Must all our anthems be written in the key
of bombs or mountains? Do you remember

when you learned to place your hand on your heart?
Do you remember when I stopped doing it

and my husband's boss told him to get
his wife in check? Where do you keep

your books, your cats, your certainty?
Would American gratitude still be ours

if it wasn't served on a table heaped with irony?
Must the turkey be opened at the legs?

Must it be nestled in its roasting pan as if asleep,
its head tucked beneath a wing? Must we talk

about crispy skin? Must we eat the organs whole?
Could we consider what it means to be sick

before we are overfull? What did you bring?
How can I help?

Have you seen my keys? my hope? my doubt?
Could you point to a question I've asked that suggests

my voice is the reason your buzz feels shot?
If you find my grace would you give it a place

to sleep for the night, feed it, and send it home?
Could someone who's not me read this out loud?

A Fact About Trees

When a branch is severed
from where it grew, the wood
still rooted in the ground
produces callous tissue
immediately at the wound,
sealing itself off the way
we close windows against
the weather. I am standing
in the empty house
where I can now only say
I once lived. The last box
has been taped shut
and carried away in a truck.
The only thing left to do
is slip off my sandals
so that even my heels, bare
and rough, will understand
this fact about trees:
the floorboards have already
begun to heal beneath us.
According to this place
that used to keep me,
I am no more than two hands
and two feet now, a bough
of five-petaled flowers
set loose by the wind.

Ambalila Hemsell

love song for the ocean

after A. R. Ammons

when you know that the belly
of the cormorant, sliced open
and full of rubbish
isn't the worst thing happening
you know too much.
the eye is drawn to the yellow bottle cap.
the rest, some mush. part of your old ski jacket and
the innards of a printer.

I love the inside part of the ocean best.
the part I can't get to. the depths, the weirdest
and wildest of it. there is no joy like the joy
of knowing I share a planet with the octopus.

what could be better than knowing there is an octopus?

every night I say this prayer:
lord, let my old toothbrushes
not choke anyone. let their poison
settle on the sea floor   an uneaten

rainbow
          invisible in the total dark.

wildfire

I

on the day of my first panic attack
the West was going up in flames

the thing I loved the most, the land
my shell, my skull was full of bees

I wept, the sluice open while
outside rainless, the cremated bodies
of trees became our only air.

I had two air filters, two children
asleep in their own rooms

I kept the windows shut but
a window opened. I saw the future
saw my father's death and
the houses all sinking to their broken knees.

I saw my chest hollowed out
like the cavity of the deer
the cougar had eaten.

her face was still beautiful
and delicate. her lashes still long.
a magpie flew out. it had been
eating the ruins of her.

I wore my silly little mask. a bird flew out
of the smoke and was dead.

the filters in the kids' rooms and the kids asleep,
I went ahead and smoked.

•

II

I lose control
of my blood

                    my heart
                    loses control of it.

the kids, marbles spilling from balloons
the balloons, pearly and pink

                    I can't drink
                    like I used to

so I smoke again

so I look into the future again
and see us relearning
to be human, humble
to animal ourselves again

my fury has
nowhere to go and

the darkest places I've ever been

weren't dark like this
inky midnight zone

something I don't want to end, over.

something I don't want to lose, lost.

·

III

in the end, not even love
will save us

in the end, we will be
eaten by houseflies

you should see how beautiful
it will be without us.

About the Authors

Abby E. Murray (they/them) is the editor of *Collateral*, a literary journal concerned with the impact of violent conflict and military service beyond the combat zone. Her book, *Hail and Farewell*, won the Perugia Press Poetry Prize and was a finalist for the Washington State Book Award. She served as the 2019-2021 poet laureate for the city of Tacoma, Washington, and currently teaches rhetoric in military strategy to Army War College fellows at the University of Washington.

AJ Dent is a poet and photographer based in Seattle, WA. Her work focuses on outdoor adventures and internal tumult.

Alli Parrett (she/her) is a queer prose writer with a Masters in Creative Writing from University of Glasgow. Her work is featured in *Allium Magazine*, *Farside Review*, *Passengers Journal*, *The Bookends Review*, and others. She lives in Seattle with her partner and dog.

Ambalila Hemsell (she/her) is a writer and educator from Southern Colorado and South India. She is the author of the poetry collection *Queen in Blue*. The recipient of a Kundiman Fellowship, a former Writer in Residence at InsideOut Literary Arts in Detroit, and a Pushcart nominee, her poetry can be found in *Fairytale Review*, *Columbia Journal*, *Narrative Magazine*, and elsewhere. Her work focuses on land, motherhood, and radical imagination. She lives in Tacoma, WA.

Carrie Redway (she/her) is a writer and mixed media artist in Seattle, WA. She is inspired by myth, folklore and ritual. Her work is published online and in print through *Really System*, *Occulum*, *Rust & Moth*, *Vulnerary Magazine*, among others.

Christina Ana Montilla (she/her) is a writer from Seattle, Washington. She is a recent graduate of the Iowa Writers' Workshop.

Courtney Bambrick (she/her/hers) is poetry editor at *Philadelphia Stories*. Poems have or will appear in journals and websites including *Invisible City* where her poem "Chicken" was nominated for Best of the Net, *New York Quarterly*, *Beyond Words*, *The Fanzine*, *Philadelphia Poets*, *Apiary*, *Schuylkill Valley Journal*, *Mad Poets Review*, *Certain Circuits*. She teaches writing at Thomas Jefferson University's East Falls campus in Philadelphia.

Deborah Bacharach (she/her) is the author of two full length poetry collections *Shake & Tremor* (Grayson Books, 2021) and *After I Stop Lying* (Cherry Grove Collections, 2015). Her poems, book reviews and essays have been published in *Poetry Ireland Review*, *New Letters* and *The Writer's Chronicle* among many others.

Erin Armstrong's (she/her) work has appeared in several literary magazines including *Mom Egg Review*, *Indy Correspondent*, *Fiction Southeast*, *Black Heart Magazine*, *Lost Magazine*, and more. She received her MFA from the University of Arizona. More of her work can be found at www.erinarmstrong.org

Harper Walton (they/them) is a PhD English student from Bath, England. Their poetry, prose and personal essays have been published by *Oestrogeneration*, *Carrion Press*, *1883 Magazine* and more. They were awarded third place for the Brick Lane Bookshop short story prize 2023. You can follow them on Instagram @harperwalton_

Jude Wineke (they/them) is a student, a book addict, and a writer of pretentious bullshit. They are from Seattle and currently live in Olympia, Washington. When they are not writing or reading, they like to draw, bike, and cook. They have never been published before.

K Janeschek (they/them) is a writer and labor organizer originally from the Midwest. Their work has appeared or is forthcoming in *Mid-American Review*, *Foglifter*, *Nimrod International Journal*, *HAD*, *The Boiler*, *Variant Lit*, *Split Rock Review*, *Poet Lore*, and elsewhere, and has won an AWP Intro Journals Project award in poetry. They live in Alaska.

Lydia McDermott (she/her/hers) is a creative and critical writer living in Eastern Washington State. Her critical work examines the development of gynecology as an oppressive discourse. Her creative work is also critical, but in a more fun way (she thinks). Her book, *Liminal Bodies, Reproductive Health, and Feminist Rhetoric*, blends the personal and fantastic with her scholarly interests in rhetoric. Her poetry has appeared in a variety of print and online publications, such as *Medusa's Laugh Press*, *Red Earth Review*, and *Prometheus Dreaming*.

Marissa Bea (she/her) is a Seattle-based editor and writer. She is working on her first set of short stories and was previously published in the last Papeachu Review! <3

Michelle Herman (she/her) is the author of four novels (*Close-Up*, *Missing*, *Dog*, and *Devotion*), the novella collection *A New and Glorious Life*, three essay collections (*The Middle of Everything*, *Stories We Tell Ourselves*, and *Like A Song*), and an advice book for children, *A Girl's Guide to Life*. She also writes a weekly column for *Slate*. Educated in NYC public schools and at Brooklyn College and the Iowa Writers' Workshop, she taught for thirty-four years at Ohio State and founded the MFA program in creative writing there.

Born London, UK, **Mikun Oluwayemi** (she/her) is a British-Nigerian self-taught visual artist with a life-long interest in photography and art. Working primarily in black and white digital photography, Mikun explores themes surrounding personhood, memory and the mundane. Her work often focuses on the emotional core of its subject or scene, exploring sentimentality and drawing commonalities between existence and everyday.

Shanda Connolly is an attorney in Los Angeles, and her fiction and essays have appeared in *Narrative Magazine*, *The New York Times*, *Prairie Schooner*, *Ruminate Magazine*, *Mosaic*, and others. In addition, her flash fiction was selected in 2021 as a finalist in the Hummingbird contest by PULP Literature, and she attended a residence last year at Millay Arts.

Vivian Li is a Seattle-based comic artist, illustrator, and storyteller. She tells funny, charming, and kind stories about occurrences both everyday and fantastic. In 2023, she published *ABC Cooking*, a comic cookbook about learning to incorporate Chinese cooking into her daily life.